Endangered
Tigers

Bobbie Kalman
Crabtree Publishing Company
www.crabtreebooks.com

Earth's Endangered Animals Series

A Bobbie Kalman Book

Dedicated by Samantha Crabtree
To Crystal Marsh, the coolest cat I know—your friendship is rare and beautiful

Author and Editor-in-Chief
Bobbie Kalman

Research
Kristina Lundblad
Amanda Bishop

Substantive editor
Kathryn Smithyman

Editor
Rebecca Sjonger

Design
Bobbie Kalman
Samantha Crabtree (cover and title page)
Katherine Kantor

Production coordinator
Heather Fitzpatrick

Photo research
Crystal Foxton

Consultant
Patricia Loesche, Ph.D., Animal Behavior Program,
Department of Psychology, University of Washington

Photographs
Erwin and Peggy Bauer: pages 17, 18, 20, 21 (bottom)
Bruce Coleman Inc.: Kate McDonald: page 28
Wolfgang Kaehler: page 27
PhotoDisc: page 21 (top)
Visuals Unlimited: Theo Allofs: page 25
Other images by Adobe Image Library, Corbis Images,
Corel Professional Photos, Creatas, Digital Stock

Illustrations
Barbara Bedell: back cover, pages 5, 6, 7, 20, 23, 25, 31

Crabtree Publishing Company

www.crabtreebooks.com   1-800-387-7650

Copyright © **2004 CRABTREE PUBLISHING COMPANY.**
All rights reserved. No part of this publication may be reproduced,
stored in a retrieval system or be transmitted in any form or by
any means, electronic, mechanical, photocopying, recording, or
otherwise, without the prior written permission of Crabtree
Publishing Company. In Canada: We acknowledge the financial
support of the Government of Canada through the Book
Publishing Industry Development Program (BPIDP) for our
publishing activities.

Cataloging-in-Publication Data
Kalman, Bobbie.
  Endangered tigers / Bobbie Kalman.
    p. cm. -- (Earth's endangered animals series)
  Includes index.
  ISBN 0-7787-1850-6 (RLB) -- ISBN 0-7787-1896-4 (pbk.)
  1. Tigers--Juvenile literature. 2. Endangered species--Juvenile
literature. [1. Tigers. 2. Endangered species.] I. Title.
  QL737.C23K344 2004
  599.756--dc22

                                                    2003025588
                                                         CIP

**Published in
the United States**
PMB16A
350 Fifth Ave.
Suite 3308
New York, NY
10118

**Published
in Canada**
616 Welland Ave.,
St. Catharines, Ontario
Canada
L2M 5V6

**Published in the
United Kingdom**
73 Lime Walk
Headington
Oxford
OX3 7AD
United Kingdom

**Published
in Australia**
386 Mt. Alexander Rd.,
Ascot Vale
(Melbourne)
VIC 3032

Contents

Tigers are endangered

Tigers are **wild** cats, or cats that are not tame. They are strong and beautiful animals, but they are in trouble. They are **endangered**. There are more than 1,000 known **species**, or kinds, of endangered animals on Earth today. In a few years, many of these species may become **extinct**. Keep reading to find out more about tigers and why they need our help.

Words to know

Scientists use special words to describe animals that are in danger. Read and find out what the words below mean.

extinct Describes animals that have died out and have not been seen for at least 50 years in the **wild**, or places that are not controlled by people

extinct in the wild Describes animals that survive only in zoos or other areas managed by people

critically endangered Describes animals that are at high risk of dying out in the wild

endangered Describes animals that are in danger of dying out in the natural places where they live

vulnerable Describes animals that may become endangered because they face certain dangers where they live

5

Five living tigers

Fifty years ago, there were many tigers alive in the wild. There were eight types of tigers. Today, there are only five types of tigers. The Bali tiger, the Caspian tiger, and the Javan tiger are extinct. They are gone forever!

Still alive

The five living types of tigers are the South China tiger, the Siberian tiger, the Sumatran tiger, the Indochinese tiger, and the Bengal tiger. They are all endangered. There may be fewer than 7,500 tigers left in the world, but it is hard to count wild tigers because they do not live near people.

South China tiger

The South China tiger, above, is the second-smallest tiger. It has short, wide stripes with big spaces between them. Of all the tigers, the South China tiger is the most endangered. Scientists believe that there are only 20 to 30 alive in the wild. These tigers are very close to becoming extinct.

Sumatran tiger

The Sumatran tiger, right, is the smallest of all the tigers. It also has the most stripes, which are very close together. There are only about 400 Sumatran tigers left in the wild. These cats are critically endangered!

Indochinese tiger

The Indochinese tiger, below, has a dark orange coat with short, narrow stripes. There are 1,200 to 1,800 Indochinese tigers alive in the wild.

Bengal tiger

There are more Bengal tigers left in the world than there are other tigers. About 3,100 to 4,700 still live in the wild. Bengal tigers, also known as Indian tigers, have rich orange coats with dark stripes. Some Bengal tigers are white with brown or black stripes. A few are **melanistic**, or black in color. There are very few white or black tigers in the wild. The tiger below is a white Bengal tiger.

Siberian tiger

The Siberian, or Amur, tiger, shown left, is the largest tiger. It is critically endangered. There are only about 350 to 400 Siberian tigers left in the wild. The Siberian tiger has a white chest and belly and thick white fur around its neck. Its orange coat is paler than the coat of other tigers.

Tigers are mammals

Tigers are **mammals**. All mammals are **warm-blooded**. Their bodies stay the same temperature, no matter how hot or cold the air or water around them is. Baby mammals drink milk from their mothers' bodies.

Striped coats

Mammals have **spinal columns**, or backbones. They also have hair or fur on their bodies. All tigers have beautiful fur coats. Most tigers are orange with dark stripes, but a few have no stripes at all.

*Tigers have two layers of fur—long **guard hairs** and soft **underfur**.*

Jacobson's organ

Do you know why a tiger often walks around with its mouth open? It is smelling with its other "nose." Besides its regular nose, a tiger has a sensitive patch on the roof of its mouth called the **Jacobson's organ**. The tiger uses its Jacobson's organ to figure out whether another tiger is male or female and if it is friendly or not! Tigers make **flehmen**, shown right, by lifting their lips and opening their mouths. They make flehmen to send scents into their Jacobson's organs.

Tigers have pink noses with big nostrils. They have an excellent sense of smell. They use smell mainly to find out information about other tigers.

*Tigers have very good eyesight during the day, but at night they can see six times better than a human can! The eyes of tigers are **amber**, or gold, in color.*

Long whiskers help tigers feel their surroundings. Tigers use their whiskers like fingers to sense nearby objects.

9

Part of the cat family

Snow leopards are big cats.

Tigers are part of the cat family. In the cat family, there are big cats and little cats. Tigers are big cats. They are the largest of all the cats.

Lions, leopards, jaguars, and cheetahs are other big cats. All big cats are wild. Little cats include bobcats, lynxes, and **domesticated**, or pet, cats.

Cats are predators

All cats are **carnivores**, or meat eaters. They are also **predators**. Predators hunt and kill **prey**, or other animals for food. A tiger uses its sharp teeth to tear meat off its prey and its rough tongue to lick the bones clean.

Ocelots are little cats.

10

*All cats, including tigers, have 30 sharp teeth for biting prey and gnawing meat off bones. Tigers swallow chunks of meat whole. They have no **molars**, or flat grinding teeth, for chewing food.*

Finding food

Tigers need to eat a lot of meat! To get meat, they must hunt other animals. Tigers that live in the wild hunt deer, elk, and wild pigs. They also eat birds, cows, monkeys, and lizards. Tigers even eat crocodiles and small elephants! Tigers are not the only predators of these animals, however. People and other animals hunt the same prey that tigers hunt, and in the same places. When too many prey are hunted, tigers cannot get enough to eat, and they starve.

Tigers are very strong, but they cannot run as fast as their prey can run. For this reason, a tiger moves as close as it can to its prey before it makes its move. It will not always catch the prey, however. In fact, tigers catch only one out of every 20 animals they hunt!

How tigers hunt

When a tiger sees its prey, it crouches low to the ground and moves silently toward it. Once the prey is close enough, the tiger rushes at the animal. It may knock the prey to the ground or pounce on it from above, as shown on the right. The tiger then uses its sharp claws and teeth to catch and hold on to its meal.

Saving the leftovers

The tiger drags its dinner into the bushes to hide it. It eats as much as it can right away and leaves the rest. If it has killed a large animal, it goes back and feeds on it for up to four days. Mother tigers share their food with their babies, but sometimes other tigers share food as well.

Tigers drink a lot of water during a meal. They drag their prey near a pool of water before they start eating it.

13

Where do tigers live?

Siberian tigers live in forests. In winter, their habitats are covered with snow.

Bengal tigers live on high, cold mountains, in dry grasslands, in marshy swamps, and in tropical rain forests. They always live near water.

Tigers live in Asia. The Asian countries in which tigers live include China, North Korea, Cambodia, Thailand, Vietnam, Malaysia, Indonesia, and parts of Russia. India, Nepal, Bhutan, and Bangladesh are other Asian tiger homelands.

Tiger habitats

Tigers live in many **habitats**. A habitat is a natural area in which an animal lives. Some tigers live in the swampy areas of steamy hot jungles. Others live in snowy forests high on mountains. Most tigers like to live near trees and water. They are good swimmers.

14

Sumatran tigers live in lush jungle habitats. They like to spend much of the daytime resting in streams. They stand or lie in the water to keep cool.

Room to roam

Tigers need to live in places where prey live. Every tiger has a **territory**, or an area of land in which it lives and hunts. Most tigers do not allow other tigers to live near them.

Large spaces

When there are many animals to hunt, a tiger does not need a large territory because it does not have to travel far to find food. When there are few prey animals to hunt, however, tigers need larger territories. They travel long distances to find food. There is not enough wild land left in which tigers can hunt. People have taken over tiger habitats to build farms and cities. (See page 24 to find out more about this problem.)

This tiger roars loudly to warn another tiger to stay out of its territory.

Marking boundaries

Tigers mark the **boundaries**, or edges, of their territories. They do this by scratching the bark of trees or by leaving behind their **scents**, or smells. A tiger leaves its scent by rubbing its face on a tree trunk or by **urinating** on a tree. Other tigers pick up the scent and know to stay away in order to avoid a battle.

The life cycle of a tiger

Every animal goes through a **life cycle**.
A life cycle is made up of all the changes
that happen to an animal from the time
it is born to the time it becomes an adult
that can make babies of its own. With
each baby, a new life cycle begins.

It starts with a cub

A life cycle begins when a **cub**,
or baby tiger, is born. Tigers
are born in **litters** of three
to four cubs. They grow
until they **mature**, or
become adults. Female
tigers mature between
three and four years
of age. Males mature
when they are four or
five years old. Mature
tigers can **mate**, or join
together to make babies.
After mating, the females
become **pregnant** and then give
birth. A pregnant tiger carries her
cubs inside her body for about 100
days, while the babies grow and develop.

*These baby Siberian tigers
are less than one week old.*

18

Female tigers have babies every two to three years. Each cub weighs about two pounds (1 kg) when it is born.

Tiger cubs

When the mother tiger is ready to give birth, she finds a safe sheltered spot called a **den**. A den can be a cave or a place with a covering of bushes. The cubs remain hidden in the den for four to eight weeks. Mother tigers change hiding places often to keep their babies safe. When mothers need to move their cubs, they pick them up by the backs of their necks. The cubs remain still while they are being moved.

Tiger cubs cannot see when they are born, but their eyes open up after one week. Cubs are born with blue eyes. As the cubs grow, their eyes turn amber.

20

Close to Mom

The cubs live with their mother for twelve to eighteen months. They **nurse**, or drink milk from her body, for three to six months. At about eight weeks of age, the cubs also start eating meat. At first, the mother hunts and brings them food. When the cubs are about six months old, they start hunting with their mothers.

This tiger cub is having its first swim. Looking at its face, how do you think it feels going into the cold water for the first time?

Fewer cubs, fewer tigers

When tiger cubs grow up, they do not stay with their mothers. They have to find new territories in which to live and hunt. There are not enough wild places for all the tigers and grown cubs, however. Sometimes the cubs cannot find safe territories with enough food. Without food, they cannot stay alive long enough to have cubs of their own.

This tiger cub will leave its mother—and its home—before the age of two. There may not be enough wild land where both the cub and its mother can find food.

A shrinking population

The **population**, or number of tigers, is getting smaller every year. There are not enough cubs to keep the population **stable**, or steady. Only about half the cubs in the wild become adults. Some are eaten by predators such as jackals, wild dogs, pythons—and adult male tigers. The cubs that do become adults may not make babies. As fewer cubs are born, the tiger population gets smaller and smaller.

Why are tigers endangered?

A long time ago, tigers lived deep in forests, and people lived on the edges of forests. In the last 100 years, the number of people on Earth has become much bigger. People began cutting down forests to make room for new homes and farms.

They took over wild lands and **polluted** the water and land where tigers lived. They burned down forests to clear land for farming. Damaging wild lands is called **habitat destruction**. Habitat destruction is a major threat to tigers.

Habitat destruction has forced tigers into smaller and smaller territories. These territories do not have enough prey for all the tigers to hunt. When there is not enough to eat, tigers must fight one another for food in order to survive.

Tigers that live near towns also face the danger of being killed by speeding cars.

Hunting tigers

In addition to habitat destruction, tigers are threatened by hunters. In the past, tigers were hunted for their coats and for sport, and they soon became endangered. Laws were passed to stop the hunting, but people called **poachers** break the law.

Poachers hunt endangered animals illegally and sell their body parts for a lot of money. They hunt tigers for their fur coats, whiskers, bones, and other body parts. The whiskers and bones are used to make Asian medicines.

Safe wild places

Many tigers live in wildlife **preserves** or parks. Preserves and parks are places where several kinds of plants and animals live. They are usually large areas. The tigers that live in these parks are free to roam and hunt. They are not fed by the **game wardens**, or the people who look after the animals. The game wardens try to keep tigers and other animals safe from poachers. They also help sick and injured animals.

*Parks and preserves provide tigers with rich habitats that are protected from poachers and pollution. Today there are 27 preserves in India alone. There are some in other Asian countries, too. At some wildlife preserves, people can go on **safaris** to see the tigers up close.*

Living in zoos

There are not enough wild places for tigers to live, so many must live in zoos. In a zoo, people are trained to care for wild animals. The best zoos have teams of scientists who know how to keep tigers and other animals safe and comfortable. They also study these animals.

Zoos give tigers a place to have babies safely. The cubs born in zoos have a better chance of survival than wild cubs have because they are protected. Some animals will not mate in zoos, but tigers will. So many tiger cubs have been born in zoos that sometimes zoos have no room for more cubs!

This Siberian cub may have a better chance to survive in a zoo, but it will never learn to hunt as it would in the wild.

People helping tigers

People all over the world are concerned about tigers. They work hard to protect tigers and help them in many ways. Some people study tigers in the wild to find out how they live and what they need to survive. Many countries have passed laws to help protect tigers. These laws punish poachers and people who buy the animal parts that poachers sell.

Groups such as the World Wildlife Fund and The World Conservation Union help raise money. The money is used to find new ways to help save tigers and other animals. Save the Tiger Fund raises money to buy blocks of land, which are set aside for tigers. These safe habitats protect tigers from poachers and provide them with prey that the tigers can hunt.

How you can help

Everyone can help save tigers. The best way to help is to learn all about tigers and their habitats. The more you know, the more information you can share with other people. Help people understand that every animal on Earth is very important to all other creatures, including people. When an animal becomes extinct, it is gone forever! Telling others about endangered tigers is a wonderful way to help. Then others can also spread the word that tigers need help!

Ready, set, go!

A fun way to help tigers is to take part in the Race for the Big Cats. You can find it at **http://bigcats.care2.com**. Every day, you can log on to the website and click on a picture of an endangered cat, including a tiger. Many companies make donations every time someone clicks! The money helps protect big cats and the habitats in which they live.

Check out tigers online!

By logging on to **www.5tigers.org** you can learn more about the five types of tigers and see some beautiful pictures.

At **www.wcs.org/adoptatiger**, you can help protect one or more tigers and get pictures of them in the mail.

At **www.nationalgeographic.com/tigers/maina.html**, you can have fun building a safe tiger home and even get to play at being a zookeeper.

To have a roaring good tiger time, log on to **www.lairweb.org.nz/tiger**.

Glossary

Note: Boldfaced words that are defined in the text may not appear in the glossary. The definitions on page 5 are based on the IUCN-The World Conservation Union's Red List of Threatened Species.

carnivore An animal that eats only meat

guard hairs Long hairs that keep water away from a mammal's skin and underfur

litter A group of baby animals born to one mother at the same time

pollute To cause harm to an area of natural environment

predator An animal that hunts other animals for food

pregnant Describing a female mammal that has one or more babies growing inside her body

prey An animal that is hunted and eaten by another animal

safari A trip across land to see wild animals in the natural places where they live

underfur Short thick hairs that cover a mammal's body and keep it warm

urinate To release waste fluid from the body

Index

2 3 4 5 6 7 8 9 0   Printed in the U.S.A.   3 2 1 0 9 8 7 6 5